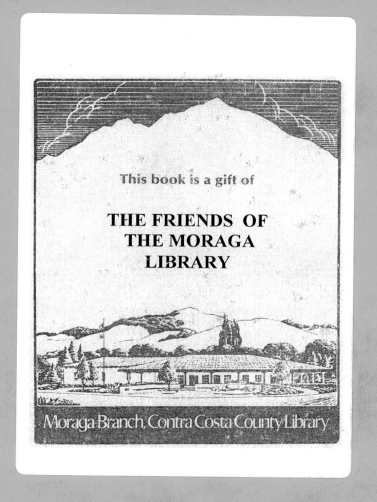

LIGHTNING
BOLT
BOOKS™

Let's Look at
Bats

Ruth Berman

Lerner Publications Company
Minneapolis

Lerner Publications Company
A division of Lerner Publishing Group, Inc.
241 First Avenue North
Minneapolis, MN 55401 U.S.A.

Website address: www.lernerbooks.com

Library of Congress Cataloging-in-Publication Data

Berman, Ruth.
        Let's look at bats / by Ruth Berman.
            p.   cm. — (Lightning bolt books™ – Animal close-ups)
        Includes index.
    ISBN 978–0–7613–3885–7 (lib. bdg. : alk. paper)
        1. Bats—Juvenile literature. I. Title.
    QL737.C5B452 2010
    599.4—dc22   2008051858

Manufactured in the United States of America
1 2 3 4 5 6 — BP — 15 14 13 12 11 10

Contents

Squeaking Bats

Folds of skin on a bat's face help the bat make squeaking sounds. Try using different faces to help you make different sounds.

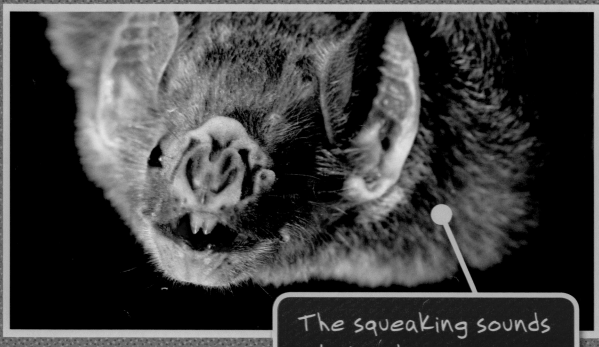

The squeaking sounds a bat makes are very high-pitched.

Are these birds? No, they are mammals called bats. Bats are the only mammals that fly.

Like all mammals, bats have hair.

Brownish hair covers this bat's body.

Like all mammals, baby bats can drink milk from their mothers.

A mother bat hangs from a branch while her babies drink her milk.

Bats at Rest

Why are all these bats upside down?

Bats hang upside down to rest.

This bat is getting ready to sleep in a tree.

Bats rest on a roost. A roost can be a tree, a cave, or an attic.

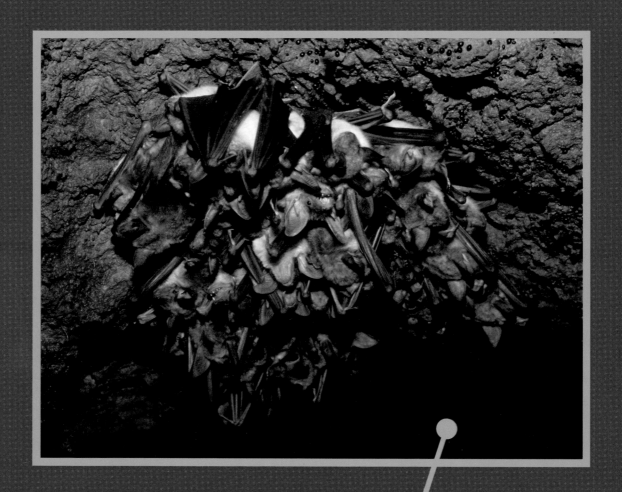

A cave makes a comfortable roost for these bats.

A bat's strong toes have sharp claws. Sharp claws help bats hold onto roosts.

Bats can hold onto roosts all day!

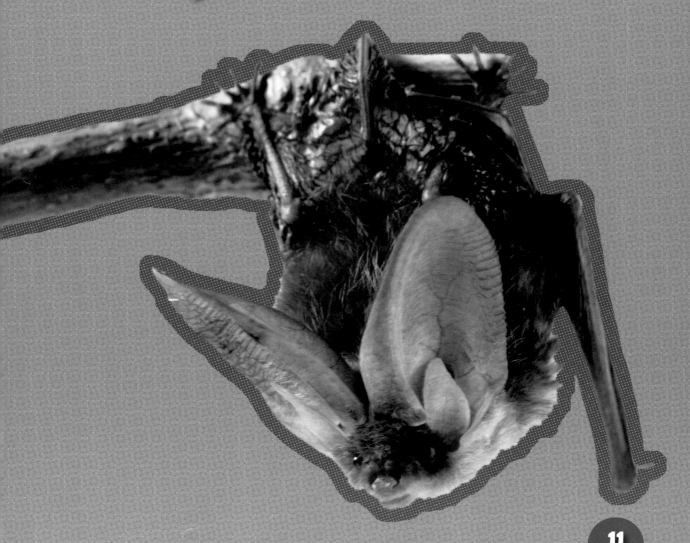

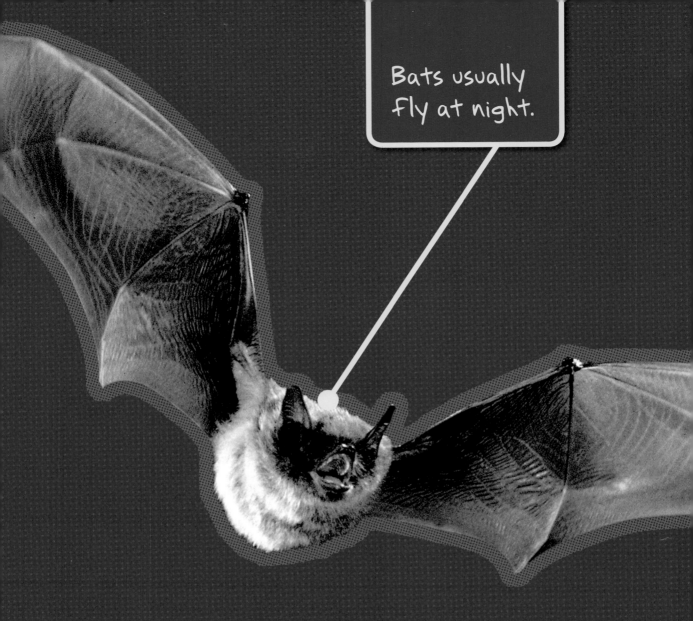

Bats usually fly at night.

Bats rest during the day. They are nocturnal. Nocturnal animals are awake at night.

Hunting—and Being Hunted

These bats leave their roosts every night to hunt for insects.

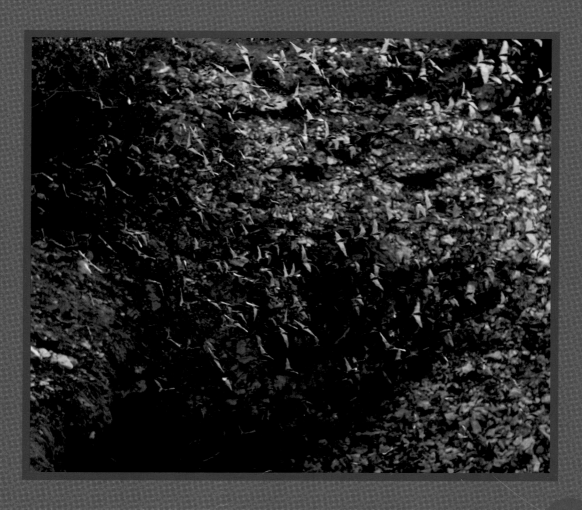

To find insects, bats use echolocation. First, a bat makes high squeaking sounds.

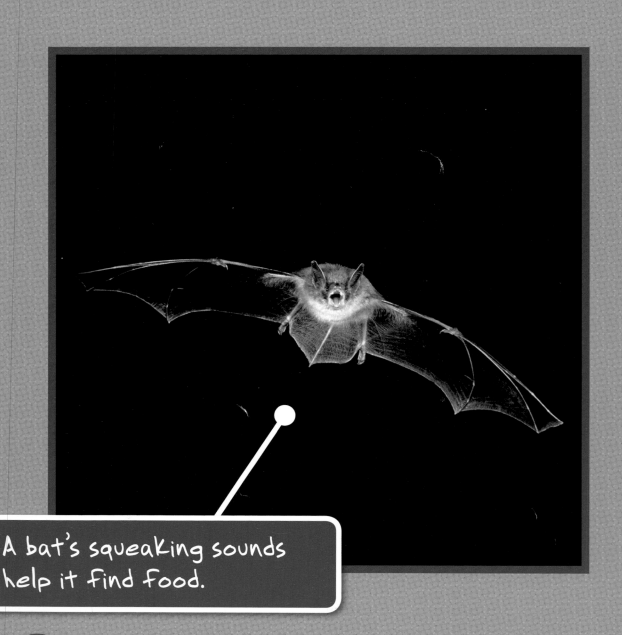

A bat's squeaking sounds help it find food.

The squeaking sounds bounce off an insect. These sounds come back to the bat as echoes.

The echoes tell the bat where the insect is. How would you make an echo?

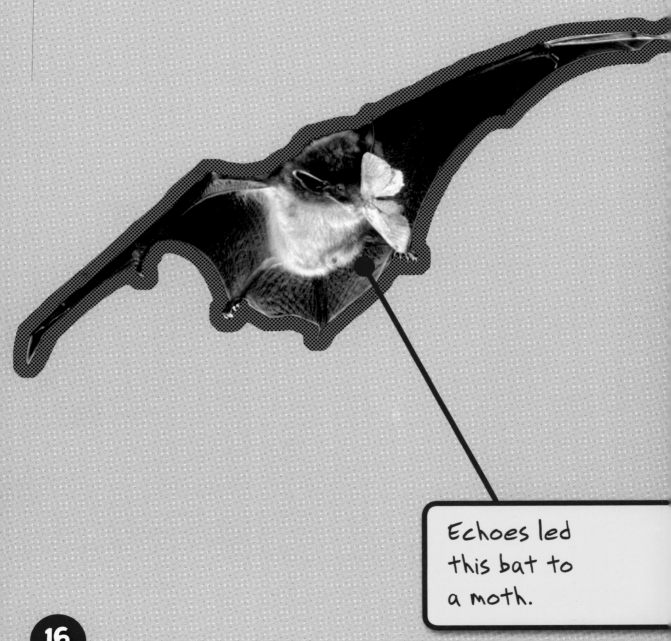

Echoes led this bat to a moth.

Some bats squeak through their noses!

The horseshoe bat squeaks through its big nose.

A bat can get a drink while flying.

Just like you, bats need to drink water.

Some bats also drink nectar from flowers. Nectar is sweet.

Bats carry yellow pollen from flower to flower. Pollen helps flowers make seeds.

Watch out!
Some snakes eat bats.

A tree snake tries to catch a bat as it flies past.

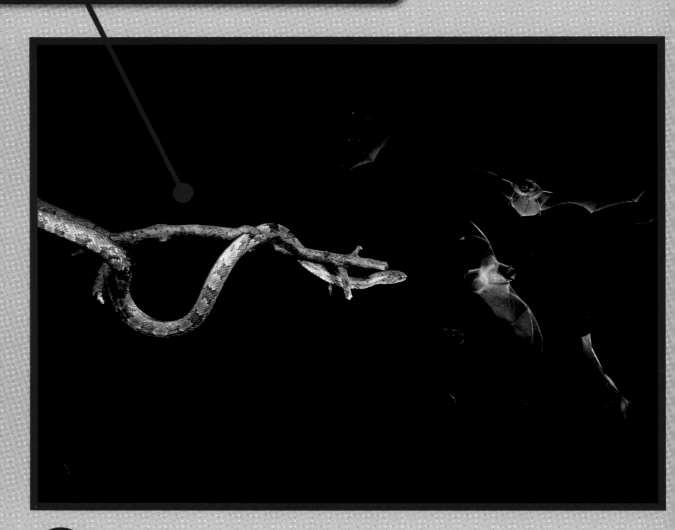

Bats' Bodies

Look closely at the wings of this bat. Each wing is made of an arm and hand.

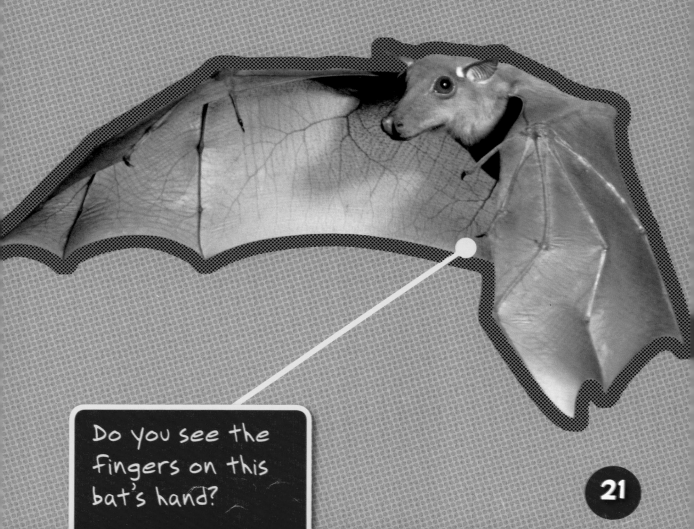

Do you see the fingers on this bat's hand?

Thin skin joins the arm and four fingers. The thumb sticks out alone.

This bat's thumb has a claw.

Baby Bats

Baby bats are called pups. Some pups live in safe places called nurseries.

These pups' nursery is in a cave.

This mother is searching for her pup.

How will she ever find it?

A mother bat knows the sound and smell of her own pup.
Look! She has found it.

The baby bat holds tight to its mother's body.

Some pups ride on their mothers' backs. **Who gives you piggyback rides?**

Pups have strong legs and claws to hold onto their mothers' backs.

Squeaking bats eat insects.
Bats also help flowers grow.
Bats do jobs that help our
whole world.

Fun Facts

- Bats live all over the world. They can be found everywhere except Antarctica.

- A bat's fur is usually black, brown, or gray—but some bats have white, yellow, or red fur.

- Bats clean their fur by licking it, just as cats do.

- Scientists have found more than 1,100 different kinds of bats.

- Bats come in all different sizes. Some are as small as your pinkie finger. Others are as big as a man!

- Only small bats eat insects. Larger bats eat plant foods.

Parts of a Bat's Body

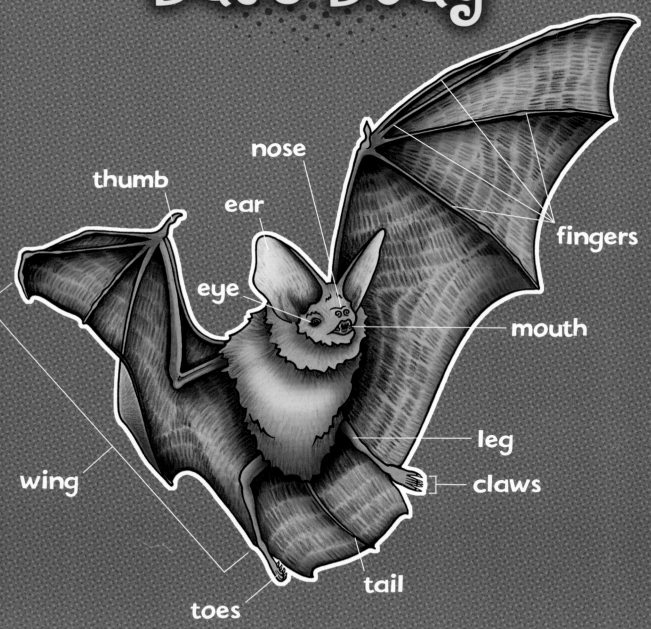

thumb

nose

ear

eye

fingers

mouth

wing

leg

claws

toes

tail

Glossary

echo: a repeated sound that has bounced off an object

echolocation: finding an object by using echoes

mammal: an animal that has hair and drinks its mother's milk when young. Some mammals are humans, bears, wolves, bats, and whales.

nectar: a sweet liquid made in flowers

nocturnal: active at night

nursery: a safe place where some baby animals grow up

pollen: yellow powder that helps flowers make seeds

pup: a baby bat

roost: a place where bats rest

Further Reading

Earle, Ann. *Zipping, Zapping, Zooming Bats.* New York: HarperCollins, 1995.

Enchanted Learning: All about Bats
http://www.enchantedlearning.com/subjects/ mammals/bat

Glaser, Linda. *Beautiful Bats.* Minneapolis: Millbrook Press, 1997.

San Diego Zoo's Animal Bytes: Bat
http://www.sandiegozoo.org/ animalbytes/t-bat.html

Simon, Seymour. *Amazing Bats.* San Francisco: SeaStar Books, 2005.

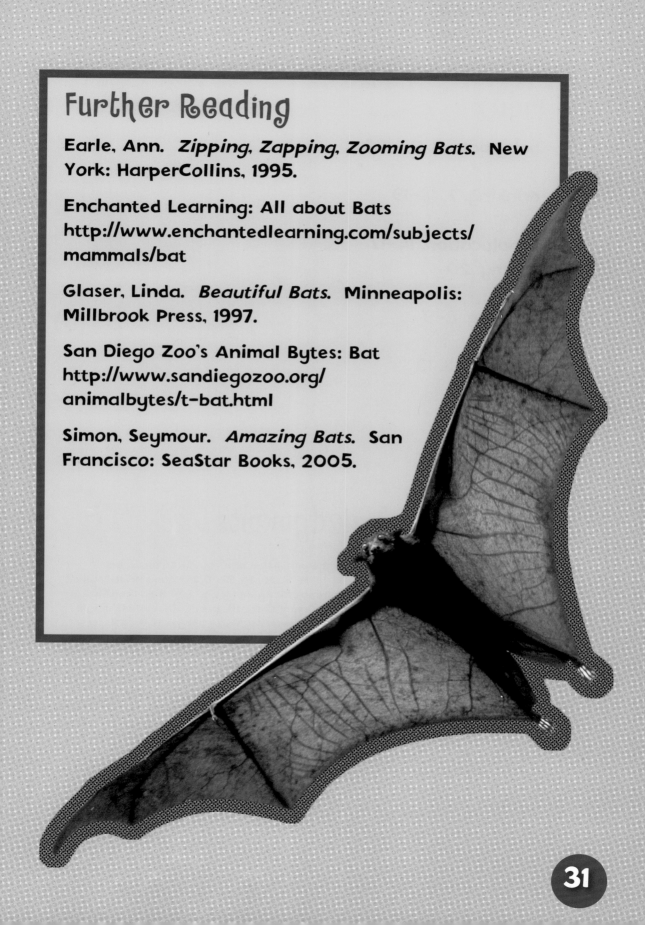

Index

Photo Acknowledgments

The images in this book are used with the permission of: © Merlin D. Tuttle, Bat Conservation International, pp. 1, 7, 12, 13, 16, 18, 20, 24, 26; © Wolfgang Heidl-Fotolia.com, p. 3; © Bruce Dale/National Geographic/Getty Images, p. 4; © Nina Leen/Time & Life Pictures/Getty Images, p. 5; © Petrp/Dreamstime.com, p. 6; © Theo Allofs/Visuals Unlimited, Inc., p. 8; © Jerry Young/Dorling Kindersley/Getty Images, p. 9; © Roger Tidman/NHPA/Photoshot, p. 10; © Frank Greenway/Dorling Kindersley/Getty Images, pp. 11, 21; © Joe McDonald/Visuals Unlimited/Getty Images, p. 14; © Jack Milchanowski/Visuals Unlimited, Inc., pp. 15, 27; © Stephen Dalton/NHPA/Photoshot, p. 17; © Charles Melton/Visuals Unlimited/Getty Images, p. 19; © Daniel Heuclin/NHPA/Photoshot, p. 22; © A.N.T Photo Library/NHPA/Photoshot, p. 23; © Les Stocker/Oxford Scientific/Photolibrary, p. 25; © Jason Edwards/National Geographic/Getty Images, p. 28; © Laura Westlund/Independent Picture Service, p. 29; © Dariusz Wiejaczka/Dreamstime.com, p. 30; © javarman-Fotolia.com, p. 31.

Front cover: © James Hager/Robert Harding World Imagery/Getty Images (top); © Martin Wall/Shuterstock Images (bottom).